The Bookbinder's Wife

and

More Poems from the North End

by

Judith Robbins

North Country Press

7/6/19

For Chuck Acker —
With gratitude for your
encouragement...
Judith

The Bookbinder's Wife

ISBN 978-1-943424-30-6

Library of Congress Control Number: 2017959349

Cover illustration used with permission by Dover Publications. From *The Artistic Crafts Series of Technical Handbooks, No. 1, Bookbinding*, by Douglas Cockerell, drawings by Noel Rooke, edited by W.R. Lethaby.

North Country Press
Unity, Maine

Acknowledgments

Animus   Jon's Hands

Church World   Fetch Me
                           Magnetism

Feminist Times   Perspective
                           Burnt Out

Grace Notes   Frozen Goldfish
                           For My Husband Missing His Cat

Maine Sunday Telegram   Giddyap!
                           At 37
National Catholic Reporter   For All AIDS Workers
                           *Footnote by a "Gifted Woman" in
                           Wm. James' *Varieties of Religious
                           Experience*
*Reprinted in *Facing Fear with Faith* under the title That the
Bones You Have Crushed May Thrill, Arthur Jones and
Dolores Leckey, Editors

Organic Gardening   These Woods Remember

Paterson Literary Review   1975: Imagine

Puckerbrush Review   Cribbing Criticism to Make a Poem
                        She Wore a Plaid Scarf

Rockland Courier Gazette   To Write What I See

2

St. Anthony Messenger	Violets: First Bruise
	St. Francis at His Post
	The Selvage Edge

The Cafe Review   Breakfast Talk

The Dudley Review   Christina's Crinum

The Worcester Review   Calendar of the Seasons
                        Worcester, Mass., June 9, 1953

Whitefield News   There They Go

I acknowledge with gratitude Dana Wilde, Careyleah MacLeod, Richard Whalen, Jane Costlow, Lucy Martin and Jack Faling for their encouragement and for their reading and reviewing of *The North End* and *The Bookbinder's Wife*. Thanks also to Patricia Newell, publisher at North Country Press; to Rob Farnsworth, a Teacher among teachers; and to my husband Jon whose love made this book possible.

To the Bookbinder

I saw within Its depth how it conceives
    all things in a single volume bound by Love,
    of which the universe is the scattered leaves.

              "Paradiso," Dante

4

Table of Contents

6

More Poems from the North End

Fetch Me

Fetch me whole into new knowledge.
Come like a fox into the henhouse.
Steal me silent out to the burning field
where torn by your perfect teeth
I'll yet yield feather on feather for your delight
until consumed, my consciousness wholly you
yet hen somehow still
reconciled to fur and stealth
remembering feather as yesterday's pageant undone.

Perspective

I pick through ashes of memories
looking for pieces that shine
odd shapes to be contemplated
something left in a pocket
and long forgotten.
Ashes remember
who handled this, and that, and when.
I hold them and hope for information.

Time is drawing short, I tell myself
people in your family die young.
Then on another day I will say,
You're only halfway through.
Variables are weather, bowels, hormones
hours of sleep the night before
the inexorable constant the moving forward
    of gray time
who drags me by the hair if I won't walk
who jangles bones and buttons in her pocket.

Giddyap!

Wolves of doubt would drag me down
hounding the sleigh that pares the ice
making tracks for other wolves to follow

close behind; I hear their breathing
red tongues swinging from open mouths.

In dreams they yawn
waiting for horses to knuckle under
the strain of the growling sleigh.

Burnt Out

Old loves hang in my mind
like unlit chandeliers.
I ask you to take them down.
I can't do it.

I've never been good at unhooking things
while balancing on a stepladder.
Something about the height and eye
and hand co-ordination makes me sick.

I need your steady hand and foot
to do this work for me. Unhook the first
and hand it down, gently, gently.
Take it slow.

I can handle the weight below
but the vertigo in the initial unhooking
is more than I can take.
Do you understand?

Then take the second and third ones down
and all the others in all the rooms.
I have boxes for them all and will send them away.
I've already made arrangements but I need your help.

1975: Imagine

Monday is diapers, baking, cleaning
house, moments snatched from elastic time
where I stand at the lift-top desk during *Sesame Street*.

Bent with urgency over the board
unable to wait for inspiration
I write the hurried thought.

In the calm remove of summer
I gather the scraps out of the desk
and build what poems I can.

John Lennon said,
Don't leave a lyric unfinished.
You won't recall the original feeling.

Imagine being a woman, John, making do
with time at hand. Then come talk to me
and maybe I'll listen.

Domestic Familiar

Kitchen cricket sings me summer
scratching sweet
my need to say, Wait

prisoner of September
locked in no cage but this house with me.
I see her not at all until it's dark

at night when she crawls the oaken floor
circling an unseen track
programmed to run

until I touch her thorax,
wondering if she has a face
how it must look when I communicate

to her black fear of something larger than she
there before her in the way
of whatever it is she wants.

Decolonization

Like a dog digging, ignorant
of that for which it digs, but smelling
something—go after it. Find it out,
dirt flying up on either side
claws tearing through rock and gravel
in a whimpering ecstasy known by dogs,
an eagerness driven by sheer not-knowing
like digging potatoes in the harvest garden
—how many, how big, the excitement builds—
like that. Like presents under the tree
and a child tearing in a fever
of getting more, more—that's how it is
with this going back to the central core
unnamed, uncolonized.

                    First, divest.
Get naked and dig. You are what you are,
whatever that is. Displace the layers
of paint and dirt, back to elementary
matter, the core as I've called it
above. Below, at center, it is to consume
the seeds—supposedly poison. Pay no attention.
It's only the apple of God. You've already eaten
in to the core. Might as well eat the seeds
and see what you see.

At 37

At 37 I began to understand
the perpetual mourning dress
of Italian women, old, shuffling
along cement sidewalks
to the shrouded hulk of St. Ann's
Church, they'd come, singly
through the gloom of Lenten
mornings, their bowed legs
and bunioned feet wrapped
in black stockings and shoes.

Before the Saint after Mass
they'd kneel, pleading their cases
worn rosaries singing in their hands.
I understand.

My Name Is Judith

My name is Judith.
I carry the head of Holofernes.
Who disputes my right to nail it
to Brooklyn Bridge or London Bridge?
I feel I could drive the nail through steel
with just my tempered fist.
I've axed that head with its matted ringlets
from my past and carry it here in a common bag.
Who could ever guess what I hold inside?

It's the Fall of the Year

The pages of my life thus far
are being torn off my spine
by a violent wind I've seen
before in dream

when pages torn
from my old bible

were flying off in every direction,
the ground beneath my feet giving way.
I grasp at what's within arm's reach
only to have it snap off in my hand.

The Bookbinder

I saw within Its depth how it conceives
        all things in a single volume bound by Love,
        of which the universe is the scattered leaves.

from "Paradiso, Canto XXXIII," *The Divine Comedy*
                                        Dante Alighieri

The Bookbinder takes me by the hand
raises me up, fending off what would kill
the writing, exposing the truth we are all
made in the image of the Bookbinder

subject to restoration by him, who gathers
the torn and spattered pages, the cover
in pieces, bitten and bent, all of it
spread on his worktable. Painstaking,

he pieces and pastes together what's
broken away from the spine, but not
lost forever because the Bookbinder
saw the book for what it was and loved it.

To Write What I See

Like Van Gogh consuming his oils
I feel I need to drop ink in my eyes
my irises crying for me to paint
words that sprint and leap through me.
I fall
grasping one
and paint it fading purple on the page.

One Art

Art is not elitist, does not
separate sheep from goats
but brings them together
      in one flock

of common vision that renders
hopeful what otherwise might
be impossibly broken or lost.

Mary Oliver Forgets

Mary Oliver forgets how many years
it's been since she first opened her hands
      "like a promise"
she would keep her whole life,
and let it go. The pipefish, that is
"back into the waving forest
      so quick and wet."

And Stanley Kunitz—
how many score of years ago
did he open his hand, and one
by one throw "perfect stones"
at "the inexhaustible oak"?
He played his game "for keeps—
for love, for poetry
and for eternal life—"

Such games these poets play—
big games, pricking their life-
blood to make it flow
onto indifferent ground.

What matters is that the blood flow,
that another poet frees a fish,
throws a stone of commitment
somewhere in the universe
whose passing thought is the ground
of being thirsty for another sip.

After His Mother's Death

The wood stove crackles this November morning
when I pick up where I left off reading in Philip
Booth's *Relations*. The "Stove" of the title
of the next poem is a Queen Clarion, Wood &
Bishop, Bangor, Maine, 1911, which stove

in his grandmother's house was a presence
the seven years' Philip and others depended
upon for heat and sustenance, for center
in winter and otherwise. It's the centennial
of that stove, I see, as I watch the mist

from early snow form mountains that move
and dissolve into air. My King stove 624
forged in Florence, Alabama, snaps
to attention when I feed it wood, as I
snap to attention when Booth feeds me

even now his pen scratching across
these morning fields, leading me into
another kingdom, whose parameters
I can not discern. They are for the nonce
clouded, as is my vision.

Cribbing Criticism to Make a Poem
For R.L.F.

I want to hear more of women talking.
You've listened closely to that,
I want to hear more.

Consider the tension between the line
wanting to go horizontal
and the weight of the poem
pulling down,
pulling out and pushing down
simultaneously.

Maybe, let the poem explode.
Then pick up the pieces and put them back together.

Don't get impressionistic
with syntax and punctuation
running sentences together around
enjambments, etcetera.
The structures deep or otherwise
of grammatical expectation and fulfillment
are useful. Through and across them lines
make one dimension of their music.

Ask yourself what's essential to motion,
to the central energy of each poem.
Pare everything else,

whatever only dresses or points away.
And remember
making metaphor is the constitution
the creation of poetic, imaginative fact
not the reconstruction of anecdote.
The poem owes nothing to what has happened.

Use the poem to find your way
back into what you thought was finished.
The poem is a radical expression of nothing ever being
finished. Poetry won't settle. Do you understand?

Palimpsest: The Cover of *James Dickey Poems 1957-1967*

He was hidden in kudzu
all these years. I never saw him
until today, limned in leaves, looking
like stone, he could be God seen
face to face, forbidden to Elijah
the prophet, but not to me,
here, James Dickey the poet
peeking through a web of kudzu
that drapes the landscape like a veil
we see through darkly to another
world behind his smile
of deliverance from fond illusion.

I beg to differ, Mr. Masters...

> *And I swear ... I never*
> *Saw a dead face without thinking it looked*
> *Like something washed and ironed.*
> *from Edgar Lee Masters' "Mrs. Kessler"*

You may never have seen a dead face
without thinking it looked like some-
thing washed and ironed, but I have
and want to tell you about the purple
rosy blue of it, my own dear father's
face that had rested quietly on a pillow
moments before he woke choking
and bleeding, dying somewhere
in his depths. Terrible sounds he made
in a quick agony of discoloration
and departure into the place where
maybe his face was washed and ironed
like the others, so he didn't stand
out in his color that frightened
all of us children around the bed.

"Young Emerging Writers Welcomed"

How about old emerging writers?
How about a word for them
crawling out from under lives
steeped in babies and trouble
that doesn't stop coming but is held
at bay with lines sneaked onto paper
after lights out for everyone else.

Yeah, how about a word for them
who have lost their looks, if they
ever had them; have published
no books: There wasn't time
in the horse race of getting supper
using an alchemy of this and that
to make a meal, a soup to feed
those babies grown. How about it?
A word for old emerging writers,
I hear their step on the stair just now.
When they come in, have them
empty their pockets, and look, look!
at the riches they've brought to you.

There They Go

The split tips of winter fingers
begins today with the left thumb.

The unrelieved chapped skin
divides with a silent sigh, only

noticed when the throb sets in
pushes up like an infant's lips

crying for sleep or food or
drink, any form of relief.

Stove Poem

This big iron box takes time to heat
On a winter morning of snow and sleet.

I huddle close in coat and hat
Then draw back slowly from where I sat

As the room heats and I disrobe
Piece by piece, mittens and coat

Hat and boots. Time to remove
the scarf, all of this foreplay

To summon the Muse from wherever
the music starts. Then to write the first line:

This box of flesh takes time to heat.

January 8

Two weeks into the light, I carry the fire
in a cooking pot from the house where I sleep
to the house where I write these lines.

The warmth of pine packed into the stove
enables me to hold the pen. I'm here again
hoping that heat and light will free

the troll within, who hunkered down
startles me with poetry, and laughs as he
takes his scarf and mittens off.

To Forgive

The trees are relieved of their ice. Today
the mercy of God dropped down as rain
at 50 degrees. After weeks below zero,
then freezing rain, ice had bent and broken
limbs off spruce, off ash and pine, snapping,
cracking, thudding down with a swish
on December snow. But that was weeks ago,
and now this thaw, one day old, enough for
the forest to lift its bent back, trees melted and
shaken free of their cold and weighty burden.

St. Francis at His Post

St. Francis has fallen asleep on the ground
outside my writing house, where he's stood
sentinel for a dozen years, the corner post
of a small garden, keeping at bay any invader
of this hallowed space where I find poems.

Granted he's fallen before, tipped over by frost
departing in spring. Fingers of ice surging
through dirt can unsteady even the greatest
of saints, but this time is different. He's frozen in.
A January series of zero nights has taken its toll

has loosened his grip on the ground. Perhaps he
tired of the pedestal. Perhaps his horizontal
position, like the reclining Buddhas of Polonnaruwa
is more fitting for a spouse of Lady Poverty

accustomed to sleeping on the ground as he was
though not in such a cold climate. Will he resurrect
in spring? I'll let that question lie with him, trusting
the answer will break through softening ground.

Don't Stick Your Hand

Don't stick your hand in the fire.
Don't do it. I knew it but did it
anyway and am suffering
        the consequent burn

from adjusting what didn't need
adjusting, fixing what hadn't asked
to be fixed, interfering with
        the burning of wood.

Let it be, but I didn't and wouldn't
and see? The blister is forming even
now. I need that thumb and will

remember through days of bandage
and aloe, to listen next time
and yes, perhaps, to obey.

For All AIDS Workers

I reached in to the fire this morning
only noticing later the burn
paining the fingers I used
to adjust a log to force the blaze.

I thought of Damien, the leper priest
scalding his feet and not feeling
the pain, but knowing the meaning
of what he saw—

To continue walking through the fire
burning his soles as never before
serving those he'd chosen to live among.

On March 14

Enough, then, of worrying about tomorrow.
Let tomorrow take care of itself.
Today has trouble enough of its own.
                                        Matthew 6: 34

On this raw day in mid-March, the Ides
tomorrow on my mind with their
not-so-veiled historical threat, I

contemplate clouds and brown fields
and see a dozen or more robins
hopping on those same fields

oblivious to Ides, and pulling worms
from the earth at a great rate.

Inventory

In mid-March I take account of the winter
scars of wood stove burns, coral badges
spotting the flesh of my fingers, hands,
wrists. And there's a fresh one, new
this morning, still white on my left
index finger, the tally-er up, pointing
the way to spring.

Last Gasp?

The sudden snow of late March
heralds the cold front that was promised,
for once arriving on time, in this place where
weather turns on a meteorological dime.

For all of March's huff-and-puff, the land-
scape snickers behind her hand because
everyone knows this strut and bombast
as limited as the flakes already a-melt.

Then, as if to give the lie, the white sky
opens. Not so fast. I'm done when I'm
done, and not a storm before.

Calendar of the Seasons

A web of spiny pain spreads in your center chest
an unwelcome guest at first, but then
in the way of pain calling full attention
to the moment, that in a moment will never
be again, you sit up straight, count your ribs,
fingers, toes, all that's given and taken for granted
with trees, birds, the marvel of song,
a child's whistle heard on a city street.

Click. The chamber was empty.
You have time to plant another garden—
whether or not you harvest it,
put down the seed, embed the transplant.
The sun is right, the rain promised
in dark clouds on the horizon—
a constant in any life that produces fruit.

Magnetism

Nails heave up from binding boards,
spring overwhelming common sense
that would hold them to their duty.

Pound them down, they're up again
unable to resist the call of her
who calls forth iron out of wood.

What fool I then, mere human flesh,
to walk in spring and feel my heart
begin to pound?

Violets: First Bruise

Fragile, purple,
faces upturned
like martyrs' faces
in Butler's *Lives of the Saints*,

sensing the crushing
foot or mower
and pleading silent
before the blade.

The Role of Lilacs

Next weekend the lilacs will be in bloom
just in time for graduation, the swelling
cones at the top of bushes reaching
toward morning sun, promising more

of the flower of poets, of old foundations
found on edges, borders—the boundary
maker for gardener and farmer, and doc-
umentarian; for Walt Whitman,

for seniors at an Eastern college, a portal
of sorts to an unseen future, its perfume
inducing a pleasant forgetfulness before
they step over the threshold into life.

Sudden Summer Rain

The rain came from some beyond
marching up through the field
knocking grasses on their heads.

Speechless before its thundering passage,
in its wake, wet and lame
lay the swollen victims.

After the Thunderstorm

The pine bundles are starry with water,
their own small lightnings
flashing in the new light.

Hail mushes underfoot
in the new heat, mosquitos so thick
I am breathing them in, a plague
for which I give thanks

in this post-diluvian world
ablaze in light, renewing
itself under a different sky.

Weeding the Garden

Weeding out the bedeviling ground cover
for the first time this spring, I see plainly
how the roots under-run the garden.

In the midst of this Sisyphean task, I reach
the peonies and therein lies the text. Ground
cover grown tall and leggy, as tall as peonies

in camouflage with pale stalks. I am not
fooled and yank it out with biblical force,
easily recognizing the tell-tale tri-leaf

top. But still I marvel at the plant's ability
to insinuate itself in the peony mound, as
throughout the garden, making me think

of C.S. Lewis' Screwtape, who knew us
humans well enough to take on the look
of a common stalk, but with invasive
roots that could easily strangle ours.

Blue Chicory

In another city where lots forgotten
between brick buildings are strewn
with trash, blue chicory thrives.
Its azure hue the color of unshed
tears, it fades to something less
than white when brought inside
and tended, seeming to need
its wilderness for survival.

In memoriam: Slugs

Luminescent traceries on the tarmac
are interconnected highways
looping borders of an unnamed land,
the sign of slugs, who unprotected
by any armor strike out on quests
leaving behind a trail of slime
that dries to glitter, solidifies to shine.
Although they perish under glare
of sun, pressure of foot or tire, a
memorial of sparkle marks the place
they passed.

Who Ever Knows?

Camouflaged among the cracks
of enamel lining the tin cup
the daddy-long-legs materialized

when the whoosh of hot tea
straightened its legs
in a line of spider pain—

dead in a moment, caught
unawares, as I was caught
and cause of its death.

Sorry, is all I have to offer.
Whether or not it's enough
who ever knows?

These Woods Remember

These woods remember when they were pasture
before the pines grew tall
before the grass trod under shadow
ceased to seem grass at all.

But still those handfuls of long green threads
like hairs on an old man's skull
send forth a promise of memory
of splendor they once knew well.

For Frozen Goldfish

How shall we speak
of these poor dumb saints,
these orange flames trapped in ice?

If Dante's right
they found their hell, who trusted
once in Providence, in the guise
of people who heavily let them down.

Christina's Crinum

My father who likes tropical plants
cross-pollinates rare plants.
My father, he's always fooling around.

The hybrid *Crinum moorei x procerum*, var.
"Christina Bauman," is a beautiful dark pink
flower he named after me.

(My mother's family are New England inbred.
My grandfather Bauman, a Swiss
came to America to be a cowboy.

He fell off his horse and broke both wrists.
Healed he returned
to being a pastry chef.)

A cross between two other crinums,
it's registered with the Crinum Society
either in San Francisco or somewhere in Texas.

And God, it's really tall.
Like a thick-stalked lily with flowers
five inches long. It's very productive.

She Wore a Plaid Scarf

What was that woman's name?
The one who lived in New Jersey
the one with straight brown hair
who started a poetry letter in her neighborhood?

Wasn't she nailing poems to posts
like Martin Luther in Wittenberg
only it was Newark and nobody cared?

And didn't she wear glasses,
thick glasses instead of lenses
and wasn't she an English major in college?

Do you know who I mean?
Are we thinking about the same person?
If you have her telephone number
I'll give her a call.

Conscientious Objection Revisited

Your photo from the jailhouse interview
summons that last summer I saw you
on the lam from the FBI, underground
on Martha's Vineyard, the date July of '65
the time, Vietnam, a war you objected to
on moral grounds, but as an agnostic, you
hadn't a chance in a culture that didn't
understand the depth of conversion you
represented. They found you, imprisoned
you for one year, and upon your release
the draft board re-classified you 1-A,
a move that moved you to publicly say,
If I am imprisoned again, I will starve to
the death in protest. This time they believed
you because they had seen your face.

A Case of Labyrinthitis
For K.K.

*In anatomy the labyrinth is a complex cavity hollowed out
of temporal bone, consisting of bony capsule and delicate
membranous apparatus contained by it; the internal ear—*

You are suffering labyrinthitis, you say.
My smile tentative, unsure if you're joking
I ask, Is it different from vertigo?

Dizziness, nausea, I've had it since childhood
but never for more than a day
you say, but this has lasted for ten days.

Your hands hold your ample head.
Your eyes come alive with describing fever
as you hold forth on the inner ear

where the internal balance of health is seared
by inflammation of that complex cavity, where
you turned and turned for explanation of how

you were feeling, until last week
when the doctor gave you the thread of that name
that led you out

and back to the edge

of the spiral subsuming your circling life
out and back to center, not

on inflammation, controlled now
by medication, but on the fire
of deeper cause.

On Being Offered a 3-Year Subscription at a Discount

I'm old and I think it wiser to buy subscriptions
a year at a time. Don't take it personally, you say
to the person on the other end of the line
who may have years of discounts yet to spend.

We wonder together whether the salesman bought
what you were selling, and share a rueful laugh at
no one's expense but our own, our age, remembering
the man who suffered from AIDS decades ago

who noted that same dilemma. Does he survive
as others do, who in the past might have died
for lack of prescriptions, and not subscriptions,
except to *Life,* and that, for how many years?

The Aging Eye Instructs

Scanning the titles in a book of poems, I read
"Learning to Knit: Bainbridge AFB." Tickled
by the thought, I conjure visions of airmen
knitting and purling, sitting in a circle of chairs
in an aircraft hangar somewhere in a war.

Maybe one is whistling, while another tells a joke
lengths of wool hanging down between their legs
sheathed in combat fatigues, ready like firemen
to move at the sound of a bell. I read the title again:
"Learning to Kill: Bainbridge AFB."

Window Death

He raised the goldfinch with exclamations
off the ground where it lay broken
delighted to find the flash of color
in the otherwise gravel place.

Its feet curled in mute submission
it didn't protest when he made it toy
to walk the wire of the clothesline tightrope
after voicing his tender wish it was still alive.

Tiring of that, down on all fours
minus one to maneuver the thing
he hopped it around to look for worms
its sealed eyes crippling it mightily for the task.

Found and Lost

A pile of clothes appeared at the roadside
as if laid out by a loving hand, cargo pants
nicely folded, white athletic socks together

one at an angle, toe to heel, and a boy's
shirt. All that was missing was the boy.
And so throughout the first week, each

day's watchful walk saw it all untouched,
until the day the pants went missing.
Shirt and socks remained unmoved. Who

cannibalized the pile? I felt a personal loss
I couldn't explain. Did the boy reclaim
the pants at his mother's behest? *They cost*

a lot! After another week had passed
I saw the socks pulled apart, the shirt
crushed into the gravel under the unmis-

takable track of a tractor, providing
the shallow grave of the kind we read about
when a kidnapped child's remains are found.

Watershed

So it's necessary to keep on shedding skin ...
We live among question marks.
        Anna Kamienska

I play at putting my hand through
a curtain, a membrane, a veil
seeking the touch of your gone hand,
and like Annie Sullivan holding Helen's
under the gushing water flowing, spilling

from that garrulous spout, you might spell
into my blind palm and so speak
into my deaf ear the language of what
you know of the other side
we spoke about through years and years
of coffee and pie and possibilities.

Jon's Hands

I was thinking about your hands again
how you handle them, and then I remembered
your father's, their knobby grace, never content
to stay in place they were always moving
touching, smoothing hair, or sorting bolts
in a loving way, the way you do, untying
knots in the children's shoes, patient
with kite strings, willing to wash
the dirty face of a doll. You could have been
a doctor with those hands, with that
unselfconscious kneeling before a child.

For My Husband Missing His Cat

I do not bring dead mouse or mole
but screws, nuts and a bolt I found
today as I walked the town roads.

I do not have fur tufts in my ears
like his or yours, my dear, but I can sleep
in the crook of your arm as he would do

when the two of you would nap as one
not stirring unless the telephone jangled
your peace, as his going has certainly done
and why I bring this metal tribute to you.

Separated by a Sail

In the woods today I thought of you
heading for the Outer Isles alone.

The weather forecast bodes well—
only a chance of a thunderstorm—
but we both know the quirks

of coastal weather, the zephyr
that suddenly becomes a blow
roiling the green Atlantic below

upending smaller skiffs caught in its grip
as we ourselves were once caught
and tossed as flotsam onto a chance shore.

So maybe you understand my concern
how I wish you safe beneath our roof
bounded by woods and subject to wind

yes, but protected by sheer tree-ness
standing between us and everything weather.

Breakfast Talk

You work at the coconut-covered donut
set in the center of a small white plate,
delicately pecking with a silver fork.

I bend the day to an early dark, asking,
Why don't you eat cereal?
Why don't you choose food that contributes to health?

Do you mind if I just enjoy it? you counter.
Absolutely! I do! False humor distills in the air.

Later I read from Henri Bergson:
> [Humanity] does not...realize
> that its future lies in its own hands.
> Man's first task is to decide
> whether or not he wishes to go on living.

> Then he must decide whether
> he wants merely to live or to put forth
> the extra effort required for fulfilling...
> the essential function of the universe
> [which is] a machine for the making of gods.

There it is, I say, after reading the piece to you.
To my surprise you respond, Exactly!
From the opposite bank of the river you
explain how eating the donut is just what makes

your life worth living, "the extra effort required
for fulfilling," reminding us both of your hedonism,
implications of which avowal I had missed before

grounded as I was in asceticism—fast, abstain,
deny yourself—I cut my teeth on such admonitions.
You, however, in wide-ranging permissions
can enjoy a coconut donut without regret,
with appreciation for another good thing of life to eat
and use to teach your wife there is more to eat
and drink and think than Aquinas ever dreamed
        in his systematics.

In the Bone House of God

No birthday I know of, no anniversary,
temperature working up to hot
grass and gardens brown with drought—

on this day the temple curtain is rent
and I return to the throne of my life
after an absence of ten years from the day that I
as a non-Jew, who had known the facts

of Holocaust but never felt them, read poems
by those who did feel them, read poems written
by those who died, and by those who survived
the horror to pass on the truth of that shadow
            that dogs the light.

I went underground that first day, not knowing
why I wept, and continuing to read the poems
until it became clear: I was in the bone house
of God, grieving with him for his own children.

Three weeks of weeping for his chosen ones,
three weeks of filling an underground lake
with tears. Three weeks of remembering day by
day the lives caught in the agony of those poems.

I never returned until today, had not even known
I was still missing, still there, deep in the earth;
a silver thread in my hand had kept me connected.

Footnote by a "Gifted Woman"
in Wm. James' *Varieties of Religious Experience*

A great Being of Power
was traveling through the sky
his foot was on a kind of lightning
as a wheel is on a rail,
it was his pathway.

The lightning was made entirely
of the spirits of innumerable people close to one another
and I was one.

He moved in a straight line
and each part of the streak or flash
came into its short conscious existence only that he might
travel.

I seemed to be directly under the foot of God
and I thought he was grinding his own life
up out of my pain.

Then I saw
that what he had been trying with all his might to do
was to change his course
to bend the line of lightning to which he was tied

in the direction in which he wanted to go.

I felt my flexibility and helplessness

and knew that he would succeed.
He bended me
turning his corner by means of my hurt
hurting me more than I had ever been hurt
in my life, and at the acutest point of this
as he passed, I saw.

I understood for a moment things
I have now forgotten
things that no one could remember
while retaining sanity.

The angle was an obtuse angle and I remember
thinking as I woke, that had he made it
an acute or right angle
I should have both suffered and 'seen' still more
and probably should have died.

Cathedral

Steady yourself with trees.
Grasp the lower branches and hold on.
Yes, like that. Greet the hemlock
without fear.

You can pass through a woods
entire this way, going from tree
to tree over rough ground,
your moving-forward steps

inevitable in a life lived beyond
the steps of what you've called
your home, and on to the home
on the other side of this great
woods you have already entered.

Don't even think about turning back.
Even now the sun is gone; darkness
settles like an old friend into your
common soul. Steady yourself
now with the presence of trees.

A Sudden Chill

A single flame when I toss
a bit of paper into the stove—

So much for our quaint lives—
a quick flash of light and heat
and then does the life burn down to ash.

Was someone warmed by my brief light?
That is the last question. I have no answer.

More Poems from the North End

For the North Enders of Poets Hill
At Annie's Book Stop, Worcester, Mass.
April 2, 2017

Veterans of other wars,
we gather in this place
of recorded history to remember

our wounds, our joys, our jokes,
our lives lived in the trenches
of the North End, where we

breathed the smoke from burning
barrels in front yards, in back yards
as we ourselves burned through

years of days. Let us pick through
the ashes of what remains and
raise up into the phoenix-light

whatever sparkles—for good
or ill—we needn't decide which
it is, only remember how it was
and render communal thanks.

It Was Worth It

Running down the field
I knew the drop at the edge
but couldn't stop.

My joy carried me into the air
and I flew 'til I fell in the trash
my foot twisted around

in a galvanized pipe. It hurt
and tickled at the same time.
I laughed and cried and lay

in the trash, calling my sister
older than I with her friend John
who were playing nearby to free me.

My mother could tell I'd been flying
again. She clucked as she strapped
the swollen ankle down.

Prescott Street

A post card came today—
a black horse with snow on its muzzle.
In the bottom left corner

Black Ice, Publishers
One Hundred Prescott Street
Worcester, Mass.

I am carried back by the black horse
to a canyon of brick echoing the click
of my child shoes as I walked home

alone from Saturday Mass, when
dread hung from factory windows
where nobody worked on weekends.

It was a tomb, a gauntlet from Grove
to North. I walked with my heart
in my throat and tried to whistle.

The envelope company's tractorless
trailers hunched against the brick
buildings, watching me as I walked past

over the tracks where sometimes a train
car stood solemnly waiting for Monday
to couple with one of its kind.

Faster past the electric transformer
fenced in by Danger. High Voltage.

Keep Out. Johnny Tripoldi didn't

and he was killed. His house was across
from the cemetery with its order and
beauty of grass and stone and avenues

named for trees: elm, spruce, maple.
I turned left onto North Street:
Noise, dogs, dirt, kids—home.

Fooling My Mother

Deep summer hung purple
from brambles in the blackberry patch
as we ate berries three at a time
grew violet mustaches and birthed freckles
in the space of an August afternoon.

Our teeth accustomed to Turkish Taffy
Bit-o-Honey and squirrel bars
we marveled at the sweetness freed
by a simple caress of the tongue.

The dropping sun reminded us
of what our mother had said,
Fill up your pails.
I'll make jam and pancakes tomorrow.

Too late. The berries almost gone
someone said, *Fill the pails with grass*
with berries on top. She'll never know.

My brain drips blackberry juice.
My fingers are stained beneath the skin.
If I squeeze my heart with my hand
it comes out purple.

A Veteran Comes to Mass: 1953

I hear him before I see him moving
from vestibule to sanctuary railing
at God knows what he shakes his finger.

The priest pauses with his back to us.
Arms uplifted like patient wings, he waits
for this railer

       bald like Elisha who called the bears
       out of woods to tear the teasing boys

to leave. Might this one too call animal powers
from beyond the doors of the sanctuary to rend
the altar boys and children who stare?

Choir quiet, congregation shifting, the railer
turns his burn-scarred face to us.
Does he wonder where he is? What army

this is that faces him down? As he stumbles
down the middle aisle, still shaking
his finger in admonition

the ushers look at the floor as he walks by.
The priest resumes the Kyrie, and the closing
door clamps off a shaft of light.

Esther's Garden

I flick an orange seed off my finger
onto the spongy ground. Immediately
memory springs up, and I see my mother's
orange trees arrayed in clay pots
on our back porch, grown from seeds
in that seedy place of dirt yards where
children played hide-and-seek, while up
above them, beyond their vision, a garden
grew. We carried that garden, pot by pot,
branches bent by new fruit, into the back
hall when frost threatened, but we never
ate the fruit of those trees, destroyed
as it was in a single night by a frost all
out of season that surprised as much as
the fruit itself and raised the threshold
of hope beyond our reach.

My Mother Never Wore a Watch
For S.S.

Time for her was that day:
Bake beans, wash clothes,
put all dreams for the future away

down at the bottom of the laundry
basket, where starched and
sprinkled shirts rolled tight

awaited the press of a hot iron
to set things smooth and right.

The Selvage Edge

I stumble on the "selvage edge"
of memory when I hear the term
spoken for the first time
since my mother explained
the bound edge of a piece of cloth,
important to know when making a dress
on the old Singer, working the treadle
as she sewed for my sisters and me

on Holy Saturday, our hair set
in rags after the bath, our shoes
set out with socks, all in waiting
for her to finish sewing and pressing
the new dresses' seams down, buttons
on. We dreamed that night in clean beds,
sheets washed and blown dry
on the selvage edge of resurrection.

Poem for My Mother While Wrapping a Gift

Make my fingers as nimble and deft
as yours were, tying ribbons, sewing
dresses, heaping meringue on lemon pie
to broil to perfect amber beads every time,
nothing left to chance when it came to
appearance. Would that we could talk now,
face to face, about those moments
that balance out others that patrol the land-
scape of memory, recalling injury without
redress, no time to seek and find forgiveness.

I admired your navigational skills
through the choppy waters of our daily life
and your dexterity at the helm. As artist
you transformed what was at hand: tin cans
to jewelry, threadbare sheet to Christmas
canvas that covered a lightning crack
       from ceiling to floor.

I see more clearly who you were and who
I am as I wrap this gift for a new baby about
to be born into this world of another time.
Send your blessing through my hands
that I might make something beautiful
       in memory of you.

Walking Home from the Girls Club, 1952

Crossing the railroad yard at dusk
scared the be-jeepers out of us, nimble-
footed though we were, crossing over set
after set of tracks shiny from regular
use that told us a train could suddenly
loom up out of the dark. We hurried then
fear making a way before and urging
us on from behind. We set our compass
true to home, still a mile to go uphill
through dead grass, broken pavement,
while headlights of cars already lit were
coming toward us: *Get out of the way!*

Worcester, Mass., June 9, 1953

The thought of it, the sight of it,
the everliving fright of it
does not die from year to year
but returns, written in memory
with a dark pen that marks black
the mind's funnel that tunnels
back to the day and night in early
June of 1953. What it meant for you
and me was fear, caught from our
mother like a dark disease, spreading
quickly through limb and vein
as we sat on the couch until very late
awaiting a second tornado authorities
warned of. Over the radio, news
of death and destruction. The numbers
grew with the passing hours—names
of the dead, names of the missing read
again and again. Does anyone listening
know the whereabouts of So-and-So?
So many So-and-So's unknown before
that night formed a terrible litany not
forgotten for months afterwards
in all our communal prayers.

An Unwitting Prophet

Bold, brazen hussy, she called me—
a teacher I admired in the sixth grade.
Struck by her words, I have never
forgotten their sound in my sixth-grade ear.

To be bold and brazen sounded original
like standing up tall and speaking your name
without shame or hesitation.

Whatever a hussy was, I wanted that too.
Given her tone, it wasn't good.
Nevertheless I wanted the content
she caught in three words: my future.

Benjamin Franklin's Epitaph wrote
by himself. —

The Body

of

Ben Franklin Printer,
Like the Cover of an old Book
It's Contents worn out
And stript of it's Lettering, & Gilding,
Lies here Food for the Worms,
yet the Work shall not be lost,
For it will (as he believed) appear once more
In a new & most beautiful Edition
Corrected and Amended

By

The Author.

Born June 6th 5706.

About the Author

Judith Robbins grew up in the North End of Worcester, Mass., in a neighborhood she celebrated in her first collection of poems: *The North End,* published by North Country Press; but for the last 50 years, she has called rural Maine home.

After raising four children, she returned to college and earned a degree in women's studies with a focus on religion. She took a course in preaching at Harvard Divinity School when she was working on a master's degree in theological studies. The experience of that class led to invitations to preach when she returned to Maine, and those assignments eventually led to a stint as assistant chaplain at Bates College before accepting a position as pastor of a community church in Newcastle, from which she is retired.

Judith can be found most days in her writing house, when the temperature is above zero.

CPSIA information can be obtained
at www.ICGtesting.com
Printed in the USA
FFOW02n1446180318
45729069-46602FF